TOLL HOUSE

SINCE 1939

Nestlé®

VERY BEST

BAKING

pil

Publications International, Ltd.

Pictured on the front cover: Triple Treat Chocolate Cupcakes *(page 8)*.

Pictured on the back cover (clockwise from top): Molten Chocolate Cakes *(page 68),* Nestlé® Toll House® Chocolate Chip Pie *(page 20),* and Nestlé® Toll House® Famous Fudge *(page 32)*.

Illustration on page 6 by Michael Jaroszko.

ISBN-13: 978-1-4127-7717-9
ISBN-10: 1-4127-7717-8

Manufactured in China.

8 7 6 5 4 3 2 1

Microwave Cooking: Microwave ovens vary in wattage. Use the cooking times as guidelines and check for doneness before adding more time.

Contents

The Beginning of America's Favorite Cookie

Back in 1930, Kenneth and Ruth Wakefield purchased a Cape Cod-style Toll House located on the outskirts of Whitman, Massachusetts. Originally constructed in 1709, the house had offered a haven to road-weary travellers, who stopped at the Toll House to pay their toll, change their horses, and enjoy a home-cooked meal. The Wakefields decided to convert it to the Toll House Inn. There, Ruth baked for her guests, and her incredible desserts began attracting people from all over New England.

One day, while preparing a batch of Butter Drop Do cookies, Ruth cut a bar of our Nestlé® Semi-Sweet Chocolate into tiny bits and added them to her dough, expecting them to melt. Instead, the chocolate held its shape and softened to a delicately creamy texture. Her recipe was published in Boston-area news-papers, and sales of Nestlé Semi-Sweet Chocolate skyrocketed. Eventually

Nestlé and Ruth Wakefield reached an agreement that allowed Nestlé to print what would become The Original Nestlé® Toll House® Cookie recipe on the wrapper of our Semi-Sweet Chocolate Bar. Part of this agreement included supplying Ruth with all of the chocolate she could use to make her delicious cookies for the rest of her life.

As the popularity of the Toll House cookie continued to grow, we looked for ways to make it easier for people to bake. In 1939, we began offering tiny pieces of chocolate in convenient, ready-to-use packages, and that is how the first Nestlé Toll House Real Semi-Sweet Chocolate Morsels were introduced.

Since they were first used by Ruth Wakefield in what would become the most popular cookie of all time, Nestlé Toll House Semi-Sweet Morsels have satisfied the chocolate cravings of millions. Today each bag of Nestlé Toll House Semi-Sweet Morsels still features this famous recipe!

Baking with Nestlé

When it's time to bake for loved ones, turn to Nestlé's family of superb baking products: Nestlé Toll House Morsels, Refrigerated Cookie Dough, & Ingredients, Nestlé Chocolatier, Nestlé Carnation Milks, and Libby's Pumpkin. For more than a century, Nestlé has provided the best-tasting products that consistently deliver high-quality taste and warm, enjoyable baking memories.

Nestlé Very Best Baking is overflowing with delicious, inspiring desserts and special-occasion cookies that are sure to rekindle sweet memories of the past. You'll find your favorite, traditional holiday recipes and some new, inspirational recipes—all triple tested, straight from the Nestlé Kitchens to yours. For hundreds more delicious recipes, baking tips, or to connect with other bakers just like you, visit VeryBestBaking.com. If you love baking as much as we do, you'll love all that this site has to offer.

Triple Treat Chocolate Cupcakes

- **1 package (18.25 ounces) devil's food cake mix**
- **1 package (4 ounces) chocolate instant pudding and pie filling mix**
- **1 container (8 ounces) sour cream**
- **4 large eggs**
- **½ cup vegetable oil**
- **½ cup warm water**
- **1⅔ cups (10-ounce package) NESTLÉ® TOLL HOUSE® SWIRLED™ Semi-Sweet Chocolate & Premier White Morsels, *divided***
- **1 container (16 ounces) prepared white frosting**

PREHEAT oven to 350°F. Paper-line 30 muffin cups.

COMBINE cake mix, pudding mix, sour cream, eggs, vegetable oil and water in large mixer bowl; beat on low speed until just blended. Beat on medium speed for 2 minutes. Stir in *1 cup* morsels. Fill each cup two-thirds full.

BAKE for 25 to 28 minutes or until wooden pick inserted in center comes out clean. Cool in pans for 10 minutes; remove to wire racks to cool completely. Frost; decorate with *remaining* morsels.

Makes 2½ dozen cupcakes

LIBBY'S® Famous Pumpkin Pie

¾ **cup granulated sugar**
½ **teaspoon salt**
1 **teaspoon ground cinnamon**
½ **teaspoon ground ginger**
¼ **teaspoon ground cloves**
2 **large eggs**
1 **can (15 ounces) LIBBY'S® 100% Pure Pumpkin**
1 **can (12 fluid ounces) NESTLÉ® CARNATION® Evaporated Milk**
1 *unbaked* **9-inch (4-cup volume) deep-dish pie shell**
   Whipped cream

MIX sugar, salt, cinnamon, ginger and cloves in small bowl. Beat eggs in large bowl. Stir in pumpkin and sugar-spice mixture. Gradually stir in evaporated milk.

POUR into pie shell.

BAKE in preheated 425°F. oven for 15 minutes. Reduce oven temperature to 350°F.; bake for 40 to 50 minutes or until knife inserted near center comes out clean. Cool on wire rack for 2 hours. Serve immediately or refrigerate. Top with whipped cream before serving.

Makes 8 servings

Note: Do not freeze, as this will cause the crust to separate from the filling.

Tip: 1¾ teaspoons pumpkin pie spice may be substituted for the cinnamon, ginger and cloves; however, the taste will be slightly different.

For 2 shallow pies: Substitute two (9-inch) (2-cup volume) pie shells. Bake in preheated 425°F. oven for 15 minutes. Reduce temperature to 350°F.; bake for 20 to 30 minutes or until pies test done.

Original NESTLÉ® TOLL HOUSE® Chocolate Chip Cookies

2¼ cups all-purpose flour
1 teaspoon baking soda
1 teaspoon salt
1 cup (2 sticks) butter, softened
¾ cup granulated sugar
¾ cup packed brown sugar
1 teaspoon vanilla extract
2 large eggs
2 cups (12-ounce package) NESTLÉ® TOLL HOUSE® Semi-Sweet Chocolate Morsels
1 cup chopped nuts

PREHEAT oven to 375°F.

COMBINE flour, baking soda and salt in small bowl. Beat butter, granulated sugar, brown sugar and vanilla extract in large mixer bowl until creamy. Add eggs, 1 at a time, beating well after each addition. Gradually beat in flour mixture. Stir in morsels and nuts. Drop by rounded tablespoonfuls onto ungreased baking sheets.

BAKE for 9 to 11 minutes or until golden brown. Cool on baking sheets for 2 minutes; remove to wire racks to cool completely.

Makes about 5 dozen cookies

Pan Cookie Variation: *Grease 15×10-inch jelly-roll pan. Prepare dough as above. Spread in prepared pan. Bake for 20 to 25 minutes or until golden brown. Cool in pan on wire rack.*

Makes 4 dozen bars

Dipped Fruit

1¾ to 2 cups (11.5- to 12-ounce package) NESTLÉ®
    TOLL HOUSE® Semi-Sweet Chocolate, Milk
    Chocolate *or* Premier White Morsels
2 tablespoons vegetable shortening
24 bite-size pieces fresh fruit (strawberries, orange,
    kiwi, banana or melon), rinsed and patted dry

LINE baking sheet with wax paper.

MICROWAVE morsels and vegetable shortening in medium, uncovered, microwave-safe bowl on MEDIUM-HIGH (70%) power for 1 minute. STIR. Morsels may retain some of their original shape. If necessary, microwave at additional 10- to 15-second intervals, stirring just until morsels are melted.

DIP fruit into melted morsels; shake off excess. Place on prepared baking sheet; refrigerate until set.

Makes about 2 dozen pieces

For a fancy drizzle: *Microwave ½ cup NESTLÉ® TOLL HOUSE® Semi-Sweet Chocolate or Premier White Morsels or Baking Bars, broken in pieces, in small, heavy-duty resealable plastic food storage bag on MEDIUM-HIGH (70%) power for 1 minute; knead. Microwave at additional 10- to 15-second intervals, kneading until smooth. Cut tiny corner from bag; squeeze to drizzle over fruit. Refrigerate until set.*

Note: *Pretzels, nuts, dried fruit, pound cake, or cookies can also be used for dipping.*

NESTLÉ® TOLL HOUSE® Hot Cocoa

½ cup granulated sugar
⅓ cup **NESTLÉ® TOLL HOUSE®** Baking Cocoa
4 cups milk, *divided*
1 teaspoon vanilla extract
Whipped cream or miniature marshmallows
(optional)

COMBINE sugar and cocoa in medium saucepan; stir. Gradually stir in *⅓ cup* milk to make a smooth paste; stir in *remaining* milk.

WARM over medium heat, stirring constantly, until hot (do not boil). Remove from heat; stir in vanilla extract. Top with whipped cream or marshmallows, if desired, before serving.

Makes 4 servings

Oatmeal Scotchies

1¼ cups all-purpose flour
1 teaspoon baking soda
½ teaspoon salt
½ teaspoon ground cinnamon
1 cup (2 sticks) butter or margarine, softened
¾ cup granulated sugar
¾ cup packed brown sugar
2 large eggs
1 teaspoon vanilla extract or grated peel of
1 orange
3 cups quick or old-fashioned oats
1⅔ cups (11-ounce package) NESTLÉ® TOLL
HOUSE® Butterscotch Flavored Morsels

PREHEAT oven to 375°F.

COMBINE flour, baking soda, salt and cinnamon in small bowl. Beat butter, granulated sugar, brown sugar, eggs and vanilla extract in large mixer bowl. Gradually beat in flour mixture. Stir in oats and morsels. Drop by rounded tablespoon onto ungreased baking sheets.

BAKE for 7 to 8 minutes for chewy cookies or 9 to 10 minutes for crispy cookies. Cool on baking sheets for 2 minutes; remove to wire racks to cool completely.

Makes about 4 dozen cookies

Pan Cookie Variation: *Grease 15×10-inch jelly-roll pan. Spread dough into prepared pan. Bake for 18 to 22 minutes or until very lightly browned. Cool completely in pan on wire rack. Cut into bars.*

Makes 4 dozen bars

LIBBY'S® Pumpkin Roll

CAKE

Powdered sugar
- ¾ cup all-purpose flour
- ½ teaspoon baking powder
- ½ teaspoon baking soda
- ½ teaspoon ground cinnamon
- ½ teaspoon ground cloves
- ¼ teaspoon salt
- 3 large eggs
- 1 cup granulated sugar
- ⅔ cup LIBBY'S® 100% Pure Pumpkin
- 1 cup chopped walnuts (optional)

FILLING

- 1 package (8 ounces) cream cheese, softened
- 1 cup sifted powdered sugar
- 6 tablespoons butter or margarine, softened
- 1 teaspoon vanilla extract
Powdered sugar (optional)

FOR CAKE

PREHEAT oven to 375°F. Grease 15×10-inch jelly-roll pan; line with wax paper. Grease and flour paper. Sprinkle a thin, cotton towel with powdered sugar.

COMBINE flour, baking powder, baking soda, cinnamon, cloves and salt in small bowl. Beat eggs and granulated sugar in large mixer bowl until thick. Beat in pumpkin. Stir in flour mixture. Spread evenly into prepared pan. Sprinkle with nuts.

BAKE for 13 to 15 minutes or until top of cake springs back when touched. Immediately loosen and turn cake onto prepared towel. Carefully peel off paper. Roll up cake and towel together, starting with narrow end. Cool on wire rack.

FOR FILLING

BEAT cream cheese, powdered sugar, butter and vanilla extract in small mixer bowl until smooth. Carefully unroll cake; remove towel. Spread cream cheese mixture over cake. Reroll cake. Wrap in plastic wrap and refrigerate at least 1 hour. Sprinkle with powdered sugar before serving.

Makes 10 servings

NESTLÉ® TOLL HOUSE®
Chocolate Chip Pie

1 *unbaked* 9-inch (4-cup volume) deep-dish pie shell*
2 large eggs
½ cup all-purpose flour
½ cup granulated sugar
½ cup packed brown sugar
¾ cup (1½ sticks) butter, softened
1 cup (6 ounces) NESTLÉ® TOLL HOUSE® Semi-Sweet Chocolate Morsels
1 cup chopped nuts
Sweetened whipped cream or ice cream (optional)

If using frozen pie shell, use deep-dish style, thawed completely. Bake on baking sheet; increase baking time slightly.

PREHEAT oven to 325°F.

BEAT eggs in large mixer bowl on high speed until foamy. Beat in flour, granulated sugar and brown sugar. Beat in butter. Stir in morsels and nuts. Spoon into pie shell.

BAKE for 55 to 60 minutes or until knife inserted halfway between outside edge and center comes out clean. Cool on wire rack. Serve warm with whipped cream.

Makes 8 servings

Zesty Lemon Pound Cake

1 cup (6 ounces) NESTLÉ® TOLL HOUSE®
   Premier White Morsels*
2½ cups all-purpose flour
1 teaspoon baking powder
½ teaspoon salt
1 cup (2 sticks) butter, softened
1½ cups granulated sugar
2 teaspoons vanilla extract
3 large eggs
3 to 4 tablespoons grated lemon peel,
   (about 3 medium lemons)
1⅓ cups buttermilk
1 cup powdered sugar
3 tablespoons fresh lemon juice

*May use 3 bars (6-ounce box) NESTLÉ® TOLL HOUSE® Premier White Baking Bars instead of the morsels.

PREHEAT oven to 350°F. Grease and flour 10-cup Bundt pan.

MELT morsels in medium, uncovered, microwave-safe bowl on MEDIUM-HIGH (70%) power for 1 minute; STIR. Morsels may retain some of their original shape. If necessary, microwave at additional 10- to 15-second intervals, stirring just until morsels are melted. Cool slightly.

COMBINE flour, baking powder and salt in small bowl. Beat butter, sugar and vanilla extract in large mixer bowl until creamy. Add in eggs, 1 at a time, beating well after each addition. Beat in lemon peel and melted morsels. Gradually beat in flour mixture alternately with buttermilk. Pour into prepared Bundt pan.

BAKE for 50 to 55 minutes or until wooden pick inserted in cake comes out clean. Cool in pan on wire rack for 10 minutes. Combine powdered sugar and lemon juice in small bowl. Make holes in cake with wooden pick; pour *half* of lemon glaze over cake. Let stand for 5 minutes. Invert onto plate. Make holes in top of cake; pour *remaining* glaze over cake. Cool completely before serving.

Makes 16 servings

LIBBY'S® Pumpkin Cranberry Bread

- **3** cups all-purpose flour
- **1** tablespoon plus 2 teaspoons pumpkin pie spice
- **2** teaspoons baking soda
- **1½** teaspoons salt
- **3** cups granulated sugar
- **1** can (15 ounces) **LIBBY'S®** 100% Pure Pumpkin
- **4** large eggs
- **1** cup vegetable oil
- **½** cup orange juice or water
- **1** cup sweetened dried, fresh or frozen cranberries

PREHEAT oven to 350°F. Grease and flour two (9×5-inch) loaf pans.

COMBINE flour, pumpkin pie spice, baking soda and salt in large bowl. Combine sugar, pumpkin, eggs, vegetable oil and orange juice in large mixer bowl; beat until just blended. Add pumpkin mixture to flour mixture; stir until just moistened. Fold in cranberries. Spoon batter into prepared loaf pans.

BAKE for 60 to 65 minutes or until wooden pick inserted in center comes out clean. Cool in pans on wire racks for 10 minutes; remove to wire racks to cool completely.

Makes 2 loaves

8×4-inch Loaf Pans: Prepare three (8×4-inch) loaf pans as directed above. Bake for 55 to 60 minutes.

5×3-inch Mini Loaf Pans: Prepare five or six (5×3-inch) mini loaf pans as directed above. Bake for 50 to 55 minutes.

SWIRLED™ Cheesecake Nibbles

36 vanilla wafers
1⅔ cups (10-ounce package) NESTLÉ®
    TOLL HOUSE® SWIRLED™ Semi-
    Sweet Chocolate & Premier White
    Morsels, *divided*
 2 packages (8 ounces *each*) cream
    cheese, at room temperature
 ½ cup granulated sugar
 2 tablespoons all-purpose flour
 2 large eggs
 1 teaspoon vanilla extract

PREHEAT oven to 350°F. Place 36 (2-inch) foil baking cups on baking sheet(s) with sides. Place 1 vanilla wafer, flat-side down, on bottom of each cup. Place *5 to 6* morsels on top of each wafer.

BEAT cream cheese, sugar and flour in large mixer bowl until creamy. Add eggs and vanilla extract; beat well. Spoon heaping tablespoon of cream cheese mixture into each baking cup.

BAKE for 15 to 17 minutes or until just set and not browned. Remove from oven to wire rack. While still warm, top cheesecakes with *remaining* morsels. Morsels will soften but will retain shape. Cool completely. Cover and refrigerate.

Makes 3 dozen mini cheesecakes

Quick Tiramisu

1 package (16.5 ounces) NESTLÉ® TOLL HOUSE® Refrigerated Mini Sugar Cookie Bar Dough
¾ teaspoon NESCAFÉ® TASTER'S CHOICE® 100% Pure Instant Coffee Granules
¾ cup cold water
1 package (8 ounces) ⅓ less fat cream cheese, at room temperature
½ cup granulated sugar
1 container (8 ounces) frozen whipped topping, thawed
1 tablespoon NESTLÉ® TOLL HOUSE® Baking Cocoa

PREHEAT oven to 325°F.

CUT dough into 20 pieces. Shape each piece into a 2½×1-inch oblong shape. Place on ungreased baking sheets.

BAKE for 10 to 12 minutes or until light golden brown around edges. Cool on baking sheets for 1 minute; remove to wire racks to cool completely.

DISSOLVE coffee granules in cold water; set aside.

BEAT cream cheese and sugar in large mixer bowl until smooth. Beat in ¼ *cup* coffee. Fold in whipped topping. Layer 6 cookies in ungreased 8-inch square baking dish. Sprinkle each cookie with *1 teaspoon* coffee. Spread *one-third* cream cheese mixture over cookies. Repeat layers 2 more times with *12* cookies, *remaining* coffee and *remaining* cream cheese mixture. Cover; refrigerate for 2 to 3 hours. Crumble *remaining* cookies over top. Sift cocoa over cookies. Cut into squares.

Makes 12 servings

SWIRLED™ Turtle Brownies

1⅓ cups all-purpose flour
¾ cup **NESTLÉ® TOLL HOUSE®** Baking Cocoa
½ teaspoon baking soda
¼ teaspoon salt
1½ cups packed brown sugar
¾ cup (1½ sticks) butter, softened
2 teaspoons vanilla extract
2 large eggs
1⅔ cups (10-ounce package) **NESTLÉ® TOLL HOUSE® SWIRLED™** Milk Chocolate & Caramel Morsels, *divided*
1 cup chopped pecans, *divided*
Caramel sauce or ice cream topping
Vanilla ice cream (optional)

PREHEAT oven to 325°F. Grease 13×9-inch baking pan.

COMBINE flour, cocoa, baking soda and salt in small bowl. Beat sugar, butter and vanilla extract in large mixer bowl until creamy. Add eggs, 1 at a time, beating well after each addition. Gradually beat in flour mixture. Stir in *¾ cup* morsels and *½ cup* nuts. Spread into prepared baking pan. Sprinkle *remaining* morsels and *remaining* nuts over top.

BAKE for 25 to 30 minutes or until wooden pick inserted 2 inches from outer edge comes out clean. Cool completely in pan on wire rack. Drizzle with caramel sauce before or after cutting into squares. Serve with ice cream.

Makes 20 brownies

NESTLÉ® TOLL HOUSE® Famous Fudge

1½ cups granulated sugar
⅔ cup (5 fluid-ounce can) NESTLÉ® CARNATION®
    Evaporated Milk
2 tablespoons butter or margarine
¼ teaspoon salt
2 cups miniature marshmallows
1½ cups (9 ounces) NESTLÉ® TOLL HOUSE®
    Semi-Sweet Chocolate Morsels
½ cup chopped pecans or walnuts (optional)
1 teaspoon vanilla extract

LINE 8-inch square baking pan with foil.

COMBINE sugar, evaporated milk, butter and salt in medium, *heavy-duty* saucepan. Bring to a *full rolling boil* over medium heat, stirring constantly. Boil, stirring constantly, for 4 to 5 minutes. Remove from heat.

STIR in marshmallows, morsels, nuts and vanilla extract. Stir vigorously for 1 minute or until marshmallows are melted. Pour into prepared baking pan; refrigerate for 2 hours or until firm. Lift from pan; remove foil. Cut into 48 pieces.

Makes 24 (2-piece) servings

For Milk Chocolate Fudge: *Substitute 1¾ cups (11.5-ounce package) NESTLÉ® TOLL HOUSE® Milk Chocolate Morsels for Semi-Sweet Chocolate Morsels.*

For Butterscotch Fudge: *Substitute 1⅔ cups (11-ounce package) NESTLÉ® TOLL HOUSE® Butterscotch Flavored Morsels for Semi-Sweet Chocolate Morsels.*

For Peanutty Chocolate Fudge: *Substitute 1⅔ cups (11-ounce package) NESTLÉ® TOLL HOUSE® Peanut Butter & Milk Chocolate Morsels for Semi-Sweet Chocolate Morsels and ½ cup chopped peanuts for pecans or walnuts.*

Oatmeal-Chip Cookie Mix in a Jar

⅔ cup all-purpose flour
½ teaspoon baking soda
½ teaspoon ground cinnamon
¼ teaspoon salt
⅓ cup packed brown sugar
⅓ cup granulated sugar
¾ cup **NESTLÉ® TOLL HOUSE®** Semi-Sweet Chocolate Morsels or Butterscotch Flavored Morsels
1½ cups quick or old-fashioned oats
½ cup chopped nuts

COMBINE flour, baking soda, cinnamon and salt in small bowl. Place flour mixture in 1-quart jar. Layer remaining ingredients in order listed above, pressing firmly after each layer. Seal with lid and decorate with fabric and ribbon.

RECIPE TO ATTACH

BEAT ½ cup (1 stick) softened butter or margarine, 1 large egg and ½ teaspoon vanilla extract in large mixer bowl until blended. Add cookie mix; mix well, breaking up any clumps. Drop by rounded tablespoon onto ungreased baking sheets. Bake in preheated 375°F. oven for 8 to 10 minutes. Cool on baking sheets for 2 minutes; remove to wire racks. Makes about 2 dozen cookies.

Makes about 2 dozen cookies

Oatmeal Chip Cookies

Razz-Ma-Tazz Bars

½ cup (1-stick) butter or margarine
2 cups (12-ounce package) NESTLÉ® TOLL HOUSE® Premier White Morsels, *divided*
2 large eggs
½ cup granulated sugar
1 cup all-purpose flour
½ teaspoon salt
½ teaspoon almond extract
½ cup seedless raspberry jam
¼ cup toasted sliced almonds

PREHEAT oven to 325°F. Grease and sugar 9-inch square baking pan.

MELT butter in medium, microwave-safe bowl on HIGH (100%) power for 1 minute; stir. Add *1 cup* morsels; let stand. Do not stir.

BEAT eggs in large mixer bowl until foamy. Add sugar; beat until light lemon color, about 5 minutes. Stir in morsel-butter mixture. Add flour, salt and almond extract; mix at low speed until combined. Spread *two-thirds* of batter into prepared pan.

BAKE for 15 to 17 minutes or until light golden brown around edges. Remove from oven to wire rack.

HEAT jam in small, microwave-safe bowl on HIGH (100%) power for 30 seconds; stir. Spread jam over warm crust. Stir *remaining* morsels into remaining batter. Drop spoonfuls of batter over jam. Sprinkle with almonds.

BAKE for 25 to 30 minutes or until edges are browned. Cool completely in pan on wire rack. Cut into bars.

Makes 16 bars

No-Bake Chocolate Peanut Butter Bars

2 cups peanut butter, *divided*
¾ cup (1½ sticks) butter, softened
2 cups powdered sugar, *divided*
3 cups graham cracker crumbs
2 cups (12-ounce package) NESTLÉ®
  TOLL HOUSE® Semi-Sweet
  Chocolate Mini Morsels, *divided*

GREASE 13×9-inch baking pan.

BEAT *1¼ cups* peanut butter and butter in large mixer bowl until creamy. Gradually beat in *1 cup* powdered sugar. With hands or wooden spoon, work in *remaining* powdered sugar, graham cracker crumbs and *½ cup* morsels. Press evenly into prepared pan. Smooth top with spatula.

MELT *remaining* peanut butter and *remaining* morsels in medium, *heavy-duty* saucepan over *lowest* possible heat, stirring constantly until smooth. Spread over graham cracker crust in pan. Refrigerate for at least 1 hour or until chocolate is firm; cut into bars. Store in refrigerator.

Makes 5 dozen bars

Holiday Peppermint Bark

2 cups (12-ounce package) NESTLÉ® TOLL HOUSE® Premier White Morsels

24 hard peppermint candies, unwrapped

LINE baking sheet with wax paper.

MICROWAVE morsels in medium, uncovered, microwave-safe bowl on MEDIUM-HIGH (70%) power for 1 minute; STIR. The morsels may retain some of their original shape. If necessary, microwave at additional 10- to 15-second intervals, stirring just until morsels are melted.

PLACE peppermint candies in *heavy-duty* resealable plastic food storage bag. Crush candies using rolling pin or other heavy object. While holding strainer over melted morsels, pour crushed candy into strainer. Shake to release all small candy pieces; reserve larger candy pieces. Stir morsel-peppermint mixture.

SPREAD mixture to desired thickness on prepared baking sheet. Sprinkle with reserved candy pieces; press in lightly. Let stand for about 1 hour or until firm. Break into pieces. Store in airtight container at room temperature.

Makes about 1 pound candy

TREASURES FOR KIDS

Quick Brownie Bites Sundaes

- 1 **package (16 ounces) NESTLÉ® TOLL HOUSE® Refrigerated Mini Brownie Bites Bar Dough**
- 4 **scoops DREYER'S® or EDY'S® SLOW CHURNED™ Light Vanilla Ice Cream**
- ¼ **cup NESTLÉ® NESQUIK® Chocolate Flavor Syrup**
- ¼ **cup whipped cream**
- 4 **maraschino cherries**

PREPARE brownie bites according to package directions. Cool on baking sheet for 2 minutes; remove to wire racks to cool for 10 minutes.

CRUMBLE 2 to 3 brownie bites into each sundae dish. Top each with a scoop of ice cream, additional cookie crumbles (if desired), Nesquik, whipped cream and a cherry. Insert 3 brownie bites into ice cream.

Makes 4 sundaes

Surprise Prize Cupcakes

         1 package (18.25 ounces) plain chocolate cake mix
      1⅓ cups water
         3 large eggs
       ⅓ cup vegetable oil
         1 package (16.5 ounces) NESTLÉ® TOLL HOUSE®
              Refrigerated Chocolate Chip Cookie Bar
              Dough
         1 container (16 ounces) prepared chocolate
              frosting
              NESTLÉ® TOLL HOUSE® Semi-Sweet Chocolate
              Mini Morsels

PREHEAT oven to 350°F. Paper-line 24 muffin cups.

BEAT cake mix, water, eggs and oil in large mixer bowl on low speed for 30 seconds. Beat on medium speed for 2 minutes or until smooth. Spoon about ¼ cup batter into each cup, filling about two-thirds full.

CUT cookie dough into 24 pieces; roll each into a ball. Place 1 ball of dough in each muffin cup, pressing it into the bottom.

BAKE for 19 to 22 minutes or until top springs back when gently touched. Let stand for 15 minutes. Remove to wire rack to cool completely. Spread with frosting and sprinkle with morsels.

Makes 2 dozen cupcakes

SWIRLED™ Around Candy Bites

80 (1-inch) paper candy cups
1¾ cups (11.5-ounce package) NESTLÉ® TOLL
HOUSE® Milk Chocolate Morsels, *divided*
1⅔ cups (10-ounce package) NESTLÉ® TOLL
HOUSE® SWIRLED™ Milk Chocolate & Peanut
Butter Morsels *or* SWIRLED™ Milk Chocolate
& Caramel Morsels
Whole roasted peanuts or pecan pieces
(about ⅓ to ½ cup)

PLACE candy cups on baking sheet.

PLACE *1 cup* milk chocolate morsels in small resealable, *heavy-duty* food storage plastic bag. Microwave on MEDIUM-HIGH (70%) power for 1 minute; knead. Microwave at 10- to 20-second intervals, kneading until smooth.

CUT small corner from bag and squeeze bag to pipe chocolate, about ¼-inch deep, into half of the candy cups. Place a peanut (if using SWIRLED™ Milk Chocolate & Peanut Butter Morsels) or a pecan (if using SWIRLED™ Milk Chocolate & Caramel Morsels) and 5 to 6 SWIRLED™ Morsels into the chocolate. Press down slightly. Melt *remaining* milk chocolate morsels in another plastic bag. Finish filling the remaining paper cups with melted chocolate, nuts and morsels.

REFRIGERATE for a few minutes to set chocolate. Store in airtight container in refrigerator.

Makes about 6½ dozen candies

Peanut Butter Jam Bars

1 **package (16.5 ounces) NESTLÉ® TOLL HOUSE®
  Refrigerated Chocolate Chip Cookie Bar
  Dough,** *divided*
3 **tablespoons peanut butter**
¼ **cup strawberry or grape jam**
1 **tablespoon all-purpose flour**

PREHEAT oven to 325°F. Grease bottom of an 8-inch square baking pan.

PLACE *14 pieces* of dough in prepared pan. Allow to soften for 5 to 10 minutes. Using fingertips, pat dough gently to cover bottom. Spread with peanut butter and jelly. Crumble *remaining* dough in small bowl. Add flour; mix thoroughly. Sprinkle dough mixture evenly over jelly.

BAKE for 24 to 28 minutes or until golden brown. Cool completely in pan on wire rack. Cut into bars.

Makes 1 dozen bars

Confetti Bars

1 package (16.5 ounces) NESTLÉ® TOLL HOUSE® Refrigerated Chocolate Chunk Cookie Bar Dough
2 cups miniature marshmallows
1½ cups (about 4 ounces) milk chocolate-covered pretzels, broken into pieces
3 tablespoons rainbow sprinkles
NESTLÉ® TOLL HOUSE® Semi-Sweet Chocolate Mini Morsels (optional)

PREHEAT oven to 350°F. Grease 13×9-inch baking pan.

PLACE whole bar of dough in prepared pan. Allow to soften for 5 to 10 minutes. Using fingertips, pat dough gently to cover bottom.

BAKE for 11 to 13 minutes or until edges are golden brown. Sprinkle marshmallows over cookie; bake for an additional 1 to 2 minutes or until marshmallows are puffed. Distribute pretzels, sprinkles and morsels over marshmallows; press down lightly. Cool completely in pan on wire rack. Cut into bars with wet knife.

Makes 2 dozen bars

Chocolate Chip Cookie Ice Cream Sandwiches

1 package (16.5 ounces) NESTLÉ® TOLL HOUSE® Refrigerated Chocolate Chip Cookie Bar Dough

2 cups DREYER'S® or EDY'S® SLOW CHURNED™ Vanilla or Chocolate Light Ice Cream, softened NESTLÉ® TOLL HOUSE® Semi-Sweet Chocolate Mini Morsels and sprinkles (optional)

PREPARE cookies according to package directions. Cool completely.

PLACE a heaping tablespoon of ice cream on flat side of 1 cookie; top with flat side of second cookie to make a sandwich. Place morsels or sprinkles on plate. Roll sides of sandwiches in morsels and sprinkles. Serve immediately or wrap tightly in plastic wrap and freeze.

Makes 12 sandwiches

NESTLÉ® TOLL HOUSE® Checkerboard

1 **package (16 ounces) NESTLÉ® TOLL HOUSE® Refrigerated Mini Brownie Bites Bar Dough**
1 **package (16.5 ounces) NESTLÉ® TOLL HOUSE® Refrigerated Chocolate Chip Cookie Bar Dough**

PREHEAT oven to 325°F. Grease 13×9-inch baking pan or dish.

FLIP each bar over on cutting board. Cut each into 12 pieces. Place pieces alternately ½ inch apart in prepared pan to make checkerboard design.

BAKE for 25 to 27 minutes or until wooden pick inserted in center comes out clean. Cool completely in pan on wire rack. Cut into bars.

Makes 2 dozen bars

Peanut Butterscotch Pretzel Snacks

1⅔ cups (11-ounce package) NESTLÉ® TOLL
      HOUSE® Butterscotch Flavored Morsels
⅓ cup creamy peanut butter
60 (3-inch) twisted pretzels
2 to 3 tablespoons sesame seeds, toasted

MICROWAVE morsels and peanut butter in medium, uncovered, microwave-safe bowl on MEDIUM-HIGH (70%) power for 1 minute; STIR. The morsels may retain some of their original shape. If necessary, microwave at additional 10- to 15-second intervals, stirring until morsels are melted.

DIP about three-fourths of 1 pretzel into butterscotch mixture; shake off excess. Place on wire rack; sprinkle lightly with sesame seeds. Repeat with remaining pretzels. (If mixture thickens, microwave on MEDIUM-HIGH (70%) power at 10- to 15-second intervals, stirring until smooth.)

REFRIGERATE for 20 minutes or until set. Store in airtight containers or resealable food storage plastic bags.

Makes 5 dozen servings

NESTLÉ® TOLL HOUSE® Mini Morsel Pancakes

2½ cups all-purpose flour
1 cup (6 ounces) NESTLÉ® TOLL HOUSE® Semi-Sweet Chocolate Mini Morsels
1 tablespoon baking powder
½ teaspoon salt
1¾ cups milk
2 large eggs
⅓ cup vegetable oil
⅓ cup packed brown sugar
Powdered sugar
Maple syrup (optional)

COMBINE flour, morsels, baking powder and salt in large bowl. Combine milk, eggs, vegetable oil and brown sugar in medium bowl; add to flour mixture. Stir just until moistened (batter may be lumpy).

HEAT griddle or skillet over medium heat; brush lightly with vegetable oil. Pour ¼ *cup* batter onto hot griddle; cook until bubbles begin to burst. Turn; continue to cook for about 1 minute longer or until golden. Repeat with *remaining* batter.

SPRINKLE with powdered sugar. Serve with maple syrup, if desired.

Makes about 1½ dozen pancakes

Sweet Pumpkin Dip

2 packages (8 ounces *each*) cream cheese,
   softened
1 can (15 ounces) LIBBY'S® 100% Pure Pumpkin
2 cups sifted powdered sugar
1 teaspoon ground cinnamon
1 teaspoon ground ginger
   Fresh sliced fruit, bite-size cinnamon graham
      crackers, gingersnap cookies, toasted mini
      bagels, toast slices, muffins or English muffins.

BEAT cream cheese and pumpkin in large mixer bowl until
smooth. Add sugar, cinnamon and ginger; mix thoroughly. Cover;
refrigerate for 1 hour. Serve as a dip or spread.

Makes about 5½ cups

NESTLÉ® TOLL HOUSE®
Cookie S'Mores

48 graham cracker squares, *divided*
1 package (16.5 ounces) NESTLÉ® TOLL HOUSE®
Refrigerated Chocolate Chip Cookie Bar
Dough
12 large marshmallows, cut in half

PREHEAT oven to 350°F. Line baking sheet with foil. Arrange *24* graham cracker squares on prepared baking sheet; set aside.

BAKE cookie dough on another baking sheet according to package instructions. Cool for 2 minutes on baking sheet. Remove cookies from baking sheet and place 1 warm cookie on each graham cracker square on foil. Top each cookie with 1 marshmallow half.

BAKE for 1 to 2 minutes or until marshmallows are soft. Immediately top S'Mores with *remaining* graham cracker squares.

Makes 2 dozen S'Mores

Marshmallow Pops

20 lollipop sticks (found at cake decorating or craft
    stores)
20 large marshmallows
  1 cup (6 ounces) **NESTLÉ® TOLL HOUSE®** Premier
    White Morsels
  1 cup (6 ounces) **NESTLÉ® TOLL HOUSE®** Milk
    Chocolate Morsels
    Decorating icing
    Assorted **NESTLÉ®** Candies and Chocolate*

*NESTLÉ® RAISINETS®, NESTLÉ® SNO-CAPS®, WONKA® NERDS®, WONKA® TART 'N TINYS®
and/or SweeTARTS® Gummy Bugs*

LINE baking sheet with wax paper.

PUSH each lollipop stick halfway through a large marshmallow; set
aside.

MELT white morsels according to package directions. Immediately
dip *10* marshmallow lollipops lightly in the melted morsels for a
thin coating. Set stick-side-up on prepared baking sheet.

MELT milk chocolate morsels according to package directions.
Repeat dipping process as above with *remaining* marshmallows.

REFRIGERATE marshmallow lollipops for 10 minutes or until
hardened. Use decorating icing as glue to decorate with assorted
candies.

Makes 20 marshmallow pops

Peanut Butter and Jelly Bars

1¼ cups all-purpose flour
½ cup graham cracker crumbs
½ teaspoon baking soda
½ teaspoon salt
½ cup (1 stick) butter, softened
½ cup granulated sugar
½ cup packed brown sugar
½ cup creamy peanut butter
1 large egg
1 teaspoon vanilla extract
1¾ cups (11.5-ounce package) NESTLÉ® TOLL
     HOUSE® Milk Chocolate Morsels
¾ cup coarsely chopped peanuts
½ cup jelly or jam

PREHEAT oven to 350°F.

COMBINE flour, graham cracker crumbs, baking soda and salt in small bowl.

BEAT butter, granulated sugar, brown sugar and peanut butter in large mixer bowl until creamy. Beat in egg and vanilla extract. Gradually beat in flour mixture. Stir in morsels and nuts. Press *three-fourths* dough into ungreased 13×9-inch baking pan.

BAKE for 15 minutes; remove from oven. Dollop jelly by heaping teaspoonfuls over partially baked dough. Let stand for 1 minute; spread to cover. Dollop *remaining* dough by heaping teaspoonfuls over jelly.

BAKE for an additional 20 to 25 minutes or until edges are set. Cool in pan on wire rack. Cut into bars.

Makes 4 dozen bars

Easy SWIRLED™ Cookie Cups

1 package (16.5 ounces) NESTLÉ® TOLL HOUSE®
   Refrigerated Chocolate Chip Cookie Bar
   Dough
1 cup (6 ounces) NESTLÉ® TOLL HOUSE®
   SWIRLED™ Morsels, any flavor

PREHEAT oven to 350°F. Grease 24 mini muffin cups.

PLACE squares of dough into prepared muffin cups; press down to make a deep well.

BAKE for 9 to 11 minutes or until edges are set. Remove from oven to wire rack(s). While still warm, fill cookie cups with morsels. Morsels will soften and retain their shape. Cool completely. With tip of knife, remove cookie cups from muffin pan(s).

Makes 2 dozen cookie cups

Note: *Try this variation! Substitute 1 package (16 ounces) NESTLÉ® TOLL HOUSE® SWIRLED™ Refrigerated Chocolate Chip Cookie Bar Dough for the Chocolate Chip Cookie Bar Dough and fill cookie cups with NESTLÉ® TOLL HOUSE® SWIRLED™ Semi-Sweet Chocolate & Premier White Morsels.*

Cookie Dominos

1 package (16.5 ounces) **NESTLÉ**® **TOLL HOUSE**® Refrigerated Mini Sugar Cookie Bar Dough
¼ cup all-purpose flour, *divided*
⅓ cup **NESTLÉ**® **TOLL HOUSE**® Semi-Sweet Chocolate Morsels

PREHEAT oven to 325°F.

CUT dough in half lengthwise; refrigerate one half. Sprinkle about *1 tablespoon* flour onto work surface. Sprinkle additional flour over remaining dough half. Roll out dough to ¼-inch thickness to form an 8½×6-inch rectangle. Cut into 12 equal-size rectangles. Place 2 inches apart on ungreased baking sheet. Score each rectangle across middle with a knife. Gently press morsels, point side down, into dough to form domino numbers. Repeat with remaining dough.

BAKE for 10 to 13 minutes or until edges are golden brown. Cool on baking sheets for 2 minutes; remove to wire racks to cool completely.

Makes 1 dozen cookies

Chocolatey Chocolate Chip Cookie Cups

1 package (16.5 ounces) **NESTLÉ® TOLL HOUSE®** Refrigerated Chocolate Chip Cookie Bar Dough
1 cup (6 ounces) **NESTLÉ® TOLL HOUSE®** Peanut Butter & Milk Chocolate Morsels

PREHEAT oven to 350°F. Grease or paper-line 24 mini muffin cups.

PLACE squares of dough into prepared muffin cups; press down lightly in center to make a well.

BAKE for 9 to 11 minutes or until edges are set. Cool in pans on wire racks for 5 minutes; remove to wire racks to cool completely.

MICROWAVE morsels in *small, heavy-duty* plastic food storage bag on MEDIUM-HIGH (70%) power for 30 seconds; knead until smooth. Microwave at additional 10- to 15-second intervals, kneading until smooth. Cut tiny corner from bag; squeeze chocolate into each cup.

Makes 2 dozen cookie cups

For Extra Chocolatey Chocolate Chip Cookie Cups:

Substitute 1 cup (6 ounces) NESTLÉ® TOLL HOUSE® Semi-Sweet Chocolate Morsels for Peanut Butter & Milk Chocolate Morsels.

Candy Shop Pizza

1 package (16.5 ounces) NESTLÉ® Refrigerated
  Chocolate Chip Cookie Bar Dough
½ cup NESTLÉ® TOLL HOUSE® Semi-Sweet
  Chocolate Morsels
¼ cup creamy or chunky peanut butter
1 cup coarsely chopped assorted NESTLÉ®
  candy such as BABY RUTH®, GOOBERS®,
  BUTTERFINGER®, NESTLÉ® CRUNCH®,
  NESTLÉ® RAISINETS® or BUNCHA CRUNCH®

PREHEAT oven to 325°F. Grease pizza pan or baking sheet.

PLACE whole bar of dough on prepared pan. Allow to soften for 5 to 10 minutes. Using fingertips, pat dough gently to form 8-inch circle.

BAKE for 18 to 20 minutes or until golden brown. Immediately sprinkle morsels over hot crust; drop peanut butter by teaspoonfuls onto morsels. Let stand for 5 minutes or until morsels become shiny. Gently spread chocolate and peanut butter evenly over cookie crust.

SPRINKLE candy in single layer over pizza. Cut into wedges; serve warm or at room temperature.

Makes 12 servings

SWIRLED™ Holiday Party Mix

9 cups oven-toasted corn cereal squares
4 cups popped popcorn
1½ cups dry-roasted peanuts
1 cup packed light brown sugar
½ cup (1 stick) butter or margarine
½ cup light corn syrup
1 teaspoon vanilla extract
½ teaspoon baking soda
1⅔ cups (10-ounce package) NESTLÉ® TOLL HOUSE® SWIRLED™ Holiday Morsels
1 package (7.5 ounces) milk chocolate-covered pretzels

PREHEAT oven to 250°F. Grease large roasting pan.

MIX cereal, popped popcorn and peanuts in large bowl. Pour into prepared pan.

COMBINE brown sugar, butter and corn syrup in medium, *heavy-duty* saucepan. Bring to a boil over medium heat, stirring constantly. Boil, without stirring, for 5 minutes. Remove from heat; stir in vanilla extract and baking soda. Pour evenly over cereal mixture; stir to coat evenly.

BAKE for 45 minutes, stirring every 15 minutes. Cool completely in pan, stirring frequently to break apart mixture. Stir in morsels and pretzels. Store in airtight container.

Makes 20 (1-cup) servings

Sugar Spritz Cookies

1 package (16.5 ounces) NESTLÉ®
TOLL HOUSE® Refrigerated Mini
Sugar Cookie Bar Dough, softened
Assorted food coloring, candies
and sprinkles (optional)
Cookie press

PREHEAT oven to 325°F.

MIX cookie dough and food coloring in medium bowl. Fill cookie press with dough following manufacturer's directions. Press dough onto baking sheets.* Sprinkle with candies and sprinkles.

BAKE for 8 to 10 minutes or until very light golden brown around edges. Cool on baking sheets for 2 minutes; remove to wire racks to cool completely.

If dough becomes too soft, refrigerate for 5 minutes or until slightly firm.

Makes about 3 dozen cookies

RICH CHOCOLATE FAVORITES

Molten Chocolate Cakes

2 tablespoons plus ¾ cup (1½ sticks) butter, *divided*
8 ounces NESTLÉ CHOCOLATIER™ 62% Cacao
    Bittersweet Chocolate Baking Bars, broken into pieces
3 large eggs
3 large egg yolks
¼ cup plus 1 tablespoon granulated sugar
1 teaspoon vanilla extract
1 tablespoon all-purpose flour
    Powdered Sugar

PREHEAT oven to 425°F. Generously butter six (6-ounce) ramekins or custard cups with *2 tablespoons* butter.

STIR *¾ cup* butter and chocolate in medium, *heavy-duty* saucepan over low heat until chocolate is melted and mixture is smooth. Remove from heat. Beat eggs, egg yolks, sugar and vanilla extract in large mixer bowl until thick and pale yellow, about 8 minutes. Fold *one-third* of chocolate mixture into egg mixture. Fold in *remaining* chocolate mixture and flour until well blended. Divide batter evenly among prepared ramekins. Place on baking sheet.

BAKE for 12 to 13 minutes or until sides are set and 1-inch centers move slightly when shaken. Remove from oven to wire rack.

TO SERVE: Run a thin knife around top edge of cakes to loosen slightly; carefully invert onto serving plates. Lift ramekins off of cakes. Sprinkle with powdered sugar. Serve immediately.

Makes 6 servings

Flourless Chocolate Cake

1⅔ cups (10-ounce package) NESTLÉ CHOCOLATIER™ 62% Cacao Bittersweet Chocolate Morsels
1 cup (2 sticks) unsalted butter, cut into pieces
¼ cup water
½ teaspoon NESCAFÉ® TASTER'S CHOICE® 100% Pure Instant Coffee Granules
⅓ cup granulated sugar
8 large eggs
  Powdered sugar
  Sweetened whipped cream (optional)

PREHEAT oven to 325°F. Grease bottom of 9-inch springform pan. Line bottom with parchment or wax paper. Grease paper.

PLACE morsels, butter, water and coffee granules in medium, *heavy-duty* saucepan. Heat over medium-low heat, stirring frequently, until melted and smooth. Stir in granulated sugar until smooth. Remove from heat.

BEAT eggs in large mixer bowl for 5 minutes or until the volume doubles. Fold *one-third* of beaten eggs into chocolate mixture. Fold in *remaining* beaten eggs *one-third* at a time until thoroughly incorporated. Pour batter into prepared pan.

BAKE for 33 to 35 minutes or until cake has risen (center will still move and appear underbaked) and edges start to get firm and shiny. Cool completely in pan on wire rack (center will sink slightly). Cover cake; refrigerate for 4 hours or overnight. (Cake can be prepared up to 4 days in advance.)

TO SERVE: About 30 minutes before serving, remove side of pan by first running knife around edge of cake. Invert cake on sheet of parchment paper. Peel off parchment pan liner. Turn the cake right-side up on serving platter. Dust with powdered sugar. Serve with dollop of sweetened whipped cream.

Makes 12 servings

Dark Chocolate Truffles

⅔ cup heavy whipping cream
1⅔ cups (10-ounce package) NESTLÉ CHOCOLATIER™ 53% Cacao Dark Chocolate Morsels
Finely chopped toasted nuts, toasted flaked coconut and/or unsweetened cocoa powder for coating truffles

LINE baking sheet with parchment or wax paper.

HEAT cream to a gentle boil in medium, *heavy-duty* saucepan. Remove from heat. Add morsels. Stir until mixture is smooth and chocolate is melted. Refrigerate for 15 to 20 minutes or until slightly thickened.

DROP chocolate mixture by rounded teaspoonfuls onto prepared baking sheet. Refrigerate for 20 minutes. Shape or roll into balls; coat with nuts, coconut or cocoa. Store in airtight container in refrigerator.

Makes 3 to 4 dozen truffles

Dark Chocolate Orange Fondue

⅔ cup heavy whipping cream
8 ounces **NESTLÉ CHOCOLATIER™**
    53% Cacao Dark Chocolate Baking Bars,
    finely chopped
1 tablespoon orange liqueur (optional)
1 teaspoon grated orange peel
    Marshmallows, fresh fruit (washed and patted
    dry), cake cubes and/or pretzels

HEAT cream in small, *heavy-duty* saucepan over MEDIUM-HIGH heat; bring to a boil. Remove from heat. Add chocolate; stir until smooth. Add liqueur and orange peel; mix well.

TRANSFER fondue to fondue pot; place over low heat. To serve, dip marshmallows, fruit, cake and/or pretzels into melted chocolate. Stir often while on heat.

Makes 4 servings (1¼ cups)

The Ultimate NESTLÉ CHOCOLATIER™ Chocolate Cake

CAKE

- 1½ cups granulated sugar
- 1½ cups all-purpose flour
- ¾ teaspoon baking soda
- ½ teaspoon salt
- 1 cup strong coffee
- 6 ounces NESTLÉ CHOCOLATIER™ 53% Cacao Dark Chocolate Baking Bars, finely chopped
- ½ cup vegetable oil
- ½ cup sour cream, room temperature
- 2 large eggs, room temperature
- 1½ teaspoons vanilla extract

FROSTING

- ⅔ cup heavy whipping cream
- 5 tablespoons unsalted butter, cut into ½-inch pieces
- 3 tablespoons granulated sugar
- 3 tablespoons water
- ⅛ teaspoon salt
- 10 ounces NESTLÉ CHOCOLATIER™ 53% Cacao Dark Chocolate Baking Bars, finely chopped
- ½ teaspoon vanilla extract

FOR CAKE

PREHEAT oven to 325°F. Grease 2 (8-inch) round cake pans. Line bottoms with wax paper.

COMBINE sugar, flour, baking soda and salt in large bowl. Bring coffee to simmer in small, *heavy-duty* saucepan. Remove from heat. Add chocolate; whisk until chocolate is melted and smooth. Cool slightly.

WHISK together vegetable oil, sour cream, eggs and vanilla extract in another large bowl until blended. Add chocolate-coffee mixture; whisk to blend well. Add *one-third* of chocolate-sour cream mixture to dry ingredients; whisk to blend well. Add *remaining* chocolate-sour cream mixture in 2 more additions, whisking well after each addition. Divide batter equally between prepared pans. (Batter will be thin.)

BAKE for 33 to 35 minutes or until wooden pick inserted in centers comes out clean. Cool in pans on wire racks for 10 minutes. Run knife around edges of cakes. Invert onto wire racks; remove wax paper. Cool completely. Spread frosting between layers and over top and sides of cake. Store any leftover cake in refrigerator. Bring to room temperature before serving.

FOR FROSTING

BRING cream, butter, sugar, water and salt to simmer in medium, *heavy-duty* saucepan over medium heat, stirring frequently. Remove from heat. Immediately add chocolate; let stand for 2 minutes. Whisk until melted and smooth. Add vanilla extract. Pour into medium bowl. Refrigerate, stirring occasionally, for about 1½ hours or until thick enough to spread.

Makes 12 servings

NESTLÉ CHOCOLATIER™
Grand Chocolate Brownie Wedges with Chocolate Sauce

1⅔ cups (10-ounce package) **NESTLÉ CHOCOLATIER™ 62% Cacao Bittersweet Chocolate Morsels**, *divided*
1 cup granulated sugar
⅓ cup butter, cut into pieces
2 tablespoons water
2 large eggs
1 teaspoon vanilla extract
¾ cup all-purpose flour
¼ teaspoon salt
½ cup chopped walnuts or pecans (optional)
3 tablespoons heavy whipping cream
Whipped cream (optional)

PREHEAT oven to 325°F. Line 8-inch square baking pan with foil; grease. *Set aside 3 tablespoons morsels for chocolate sauce.*

HEAT *1 cup* morsels, sugar, butter and water in small, *heavy-duty* saucepan over low heat, stirring constantly until morsels and butter are melted. Pour into medium bowl. Stir in eggs, 1 at a time, until mixed in. Stir in vanilla extract. Add flour and salt; stir well. Stir in *remaining* morsels (*except sauce morsels*) and nuts, if desired. Pour into prepared baking pan.

BAKE for 33 to 35 minutes or until wooden pick inserted in center comes out slightly sticky. Cool in pan on wire rack. Lift brownie from pan with foil to cutting board. Carefully remove foil. Cut brownie square in half. Cut each half into thirds for a total of 6 pieces. Cut each piece in half diagonally to form triangles for a total of 12.

PLACE cream in small, uncovered, microwave-safe dish. Microwave on HIGH (100%) power for 25 to 30 seconds. Add *reserved 3 tablespoons* of morsels; stir until smooth. (Sauce will thicken as it cools.) Place wedge on serving plate; top or drizzle with a teaspoon of sauce. Top with whipped cream, if desired.

Makes 12 servings

SAVORY AND SATISFYING

Pumpkin Chili Mexicana

2   tablespoons vegetable oil
½   cup chopped onion
1   cup (1 large) chopped red or green bell pepper
1   clove garlic, finely chopped
1   pound ground turkey
2   cans (14.5 ounces *each*) no-salt-added diced
     tomatoes, undrained
1   can (15 ounces) LIBBY'S® 100% Pure Pumpkin
1   can (15 ounces) tomato sauce
1   can (15¼ ounces) kidney beans, drained
1   can (4 ounces) diced green chiles
½   cup loose-pack frozen whole kernel corn
1   tablespoon chili powder
1   teaspoon ground cumin
½   teaspoon ground black pepper

HEAT vegetable oil in large saucepan over medium-high heat.
Add onion, bell pepper and garlic; cook, stirring frequently, for 5 to
7 minutes or until tender. Add turkey; cook until browned. Drain.

ADD tomatoes with juice, pumpkin, tomato sauce, beans, chiles,
corn, chili powder, cumin and black pepper. Bring to a boil. Reduce
heat to low. Cover; cook, stirring occasionally, for 30 minutes.

Makes 6 to 8 servings

Cranberry-Dressed Mixed Greens with Apples & Glazed Pecans

DRESSING

⅔ cup (5 fluid-ounce can) NESTLÉ® CARNATION® Fat Free Evaporated Milk

½ cup sweetened dried cranberries

3 tablespoons mayonnaise

3 tablespoons cranberry juice concentrate

2 teaspoons lemon juice

1 small clove garlic, finely chopped (optional)

¼ teaspoon salt

¼ teaspoon ground black pepper

½ teaspoon dried tarragon leaves

SALAD

6 cups (about 5.5-ounce bag) mixed baby greens

2 tart apples (such as Granny Smith), cored, diced

½ cup sweetened dried cranberries

½ cup glazed pecans

FOR DRESSING

PLACE evaporated milk, cranberries, mayonnaise, cranberry juice concentrate, lemon juice, garlic, salt and black pepper in blender; cover. Process until combined. Stir in tarragon. Makes 1¼ cups.

FOR SALAD

COMBINE greens, apples, cranberries and *1 cup* dressing in large bowl. Sprinkle with pecans. Serve with remaining dressing, if desired.

Makes 4 servings

Cooking Tip: *For a heartier salad, add diced, cooked turkey.*

Creamy Chicken and Rice Bake

   1 can (12 fluid ounces) NESTLÉ® CARNATION®
         Evaporated Milk
   1 package (3 ounces) cream cheese, softened
   1 can (10¾ ounces) cream of chicken soup
   ½ cup water
   ½ teaspoon garlic powder
   ⅛ teaspoon ground black pepper
   1 bag (16 ounces) frozen broccoli, cauliflower and
         carrot mix, thawed
   2 cups cubed, precooked chicken
   1½ cups uncooked instant white rice
   ½ cup (2 ounces) shredded mild Cheddar cheese

PREHEAT oven to 350°F. Grease 13×9-inch baking dish.

COMBINE evaporated milk and cream cheese in baking dish with wire whisk until smooth. Add soup, water, garlic powder and black pepper; mix well. Add vegetables, chicken and rice. Cover tightly with foil.

BAKE for 35 minutes. Remove cover and top with cheese. Continue baking uncovered for 10 to 15 minutes or until cheese is melted and mixture is bubbly. Let stand 5 minutes before serving.

Makes 8 to 10 servings

Baked Potato Soup

¼ cup (½ stick) butter or margarine
¼ cup chopped onion
¼ cup all-purpose flour
1 can (14.5 fluid ounces) chicken broth
1 can (12 fluid ounces) NESTLÉ® CARNATION®
    Evaporated Milk
2 large or 3 medium baking potatoes, baked or
    microwaved
   Cooked and crumbled bacon (optional)
   Shredded Cheddar cheese (optional)
   Sliced green onions (optional)

MELT butter in large saucepan over medium heat. Add onion;
cook, stirring occasionally, for 1 to 2 minutes or until tender. Stir
in flour. Gradually stir in broth and evaporated milk. Scoop potato
pulp from *1* potato (reserve potato skin); mash. Add pulp to broth
mixture. Cook over medium heat, stirring occasionally, until
mixture comes to a boil. Dice *remaining* potato skin and potato(es);
add to soup. Heat through. Season with salt and ground black
pepper. Top each serving with bacon, cheese and green onions, if
desired.

Makes 4 servings

Variation: *For a different twist to this recipe, omit the bacon, Cheddar cheese
and green onions. Cook 2 tablespoons shredded carrot with the onion and
add ¼ teaspoon dried dill to the soup when adding the broth. Proceed as
above.*

Spicy Jac Mac & Cheese with Broccoli

- 2 cups (8 ounces) dry elbow macaroni
- 2 cups chopped frozen or fresh broccoli
- 2 cups (8 ounces) shredded sharp Cheddar cheese
- 2 cups (8 ounces) shredded Pepper Jack cheese*
- 1 can (12 fluid ounces) **NESTLÉ® CARNATION®** Evaporated Milk
- ½ cup grated Parmesan cheese, *divided*
- ½ teaspoon ground black pepper
- 2 tablespoons bread crumbs

For a less spicy version, substitute 2 cups (8 ounces) shredded Monterey Jack cheese and a few dashes of hot pepper sauce (optional) for Pepper Jack cheese.

PREHEAT oven to 350°F. Lightly butter 2½-quart casserole dish.

COOK macaroni in large saucepan according to package directions, adding broccoli to boiling pasta water for last 3 minutes of cooking time; drain.

COMBINE cooked pasta, broccoli, Cheddar cheese, Pepper Jack cheese, evaporated milk, ¼ *cup* Parmesan cheese and black pepper in large bowl. Pour into prepared casserole dish. Combine *remaining* Parmesan cheese and bread crumbs; sprinkle over macaroni mixture. Cover tightly with aluminum foil.

BAKE covered for 20 minutes. Remove foil; bake for additional 10 minutes or until lightly browned.

Makes 8 servings

Ham and Swiss Quiche

- 1 *unbaked* 9-inch (4-cup volume) deep-dish pie shell
- 1 cup (4-ounces) shredded Swiss cheese, *divided*
- 1 cup finely chopped cooked ham
- 2 green onions, sliced
- 1 can (12-fluid ounces) NESTLÉ® CARNATION® Evaporated Milk
- 3 large eggs
- ¼ cup all-purpose flour
- ¼ teaspoon salt
- ⅛ teaspoon ground black pepper

PREHEAT oven to 350°F.

SPRINKLE *½ cup* cheese, ham and green onions into pie crust. Whisk together evaporated milk, eggs, flour, salt and black pepper in large bowl. Pour mixture into pie shell; sprinkle with *remaining* cheese.

BAKE for 45 to 50 minutes or until knife inserted near center comes out clean. Cool on wire rack for 10 minutes before serving.

Makes 8 servings

For Mini Quiche Appetizers: *Use 1½ packages (3 crusts) refrigerated pie crusts. Grease miniature muffin pans. Unfold crust on lightly floured surface. Cut 14 (2½-inch) circles from each crust. Press 1 circle of dough into bottom and up side of each cup. Repeat with remaining crusts. Combine cheese, ham, green onions, ⅔ cup (5 fluid-ounce can) NESTLÉ® CARNATION® Evaporated Milk, 2 eggs (lightly beaten), 2 tablespoons flour, salt and black pepper in large bowl; mix well. Spoon mixture into crusts, filling three-fourths full. Bake in preheated 350°F. oven for 20 to 25 minutes or until crusts are golden brown. Cool slightly; lift quiche from cup with tip of knife. Serve warm or cool and freeze for later entertaining. Makes 3½ dozen.*

Hash Brown Casserole

3 cartons (4 ounces *each*) cholesterol-free egg
  product or 6 large eggs, well beaten
1 can (12 fluid ounces) NESTLÉ® CARNATION®
  Evaporated Milk
1 teaspoon salt
½ teaspoon ground black pepper
1 package (30 ounces) frozen shredded hash
  brown potatoes
2 cups (8 ounces) shredded Cheddar cheese
1 medium onion, chopped
1 small green bell pepper, chopped
1 cup diced ham (optional)

PREHEAT oven to 350°F. Grease 13×9-inch baking dish.

COMBINE egg product, evaporated milk, salt and black pepper in large bowl. Add potatoes, cheese, onion, bell pepper and ham; mix well. Pour mixture into prepared baking dish.

BAKE for 60 to 65 minutes or until set.

Makes 12 servings

Note: *For a lower fat version of this recipe, use cholesterol-free egg product, substitute NESTLÉ® CARNATION® Evaporated Fat Free Milk for Evaporated Milk and 10 slices turkey bacon, cooked and chopped, for the diced ham. Proceed as above.*

Sweet & White Scalloped Potatoes with Parmesan & Thyme

1 can (12 fluid ounces) NESTLÉ® CARNATION®
    Evaporated Milk
2 MAGGI® Reduced Sodium Chicken Flavor
    Bouillon Cubes
1 teaspoon onion powder
½ teaspoon dried thyme leaves
4 cups (1½ pounds) potatoes, peeled, cut into
    ¼-inch slices
2 cups (½ pound) sweet potatoes or yams, peeled,
    cut into ¼-inch slices
½ cup grated Parmesan cheese

HEAT evaporated milk, bouillon cubes, onion powder and thyme in large skillet over medium high heat, stirring occasionally until mixture comes to a boil and bouillon is dissolved. Add potatoes.

COOK, stirring occasionally, until mixture comes to boil. Cover; reduce heat to low. Cook, rearranging potatoes gently and occasionally, for 35 to 40 minutes or until potatoes are tender. Sprinkle with cheese; serve immediately.

Makes 8 servings

Cooking Tip: *For quick and consistently thin potato slices, use the slicing blade of a food processor.*